50 TH

BOOK SERIES
REVIEWS FROM READERS

I recently downloaded a couple of books from this series to read over the weekend thinking I would read just one or two. However, I so loved the books that I read all the six books I had downloaded in one go and ended up downloading a few more today. Written by different authors, the books offer practical advice on how you can perform or achieve certain goals in life, which in this case is how to have a better life.

The information is simple to digest and learn from, and is incredibly useful. There are also resources listed at the end of the book that you can use to get more information.

50 Things To Know To Have A Better Life: Self-Improvement Made Easy!

Author Dannii Cohen

This book is very helpful and provides simple tips on how to improve your everyday life. I found it to be useful in improving my overall attitude.

50 Things to Know For Your Mindfulness & Meditation Journey Author Nina Edmondso

---

Quick read with 50 short and easy tips for what to think about before starting to homeschool.

50 Things to Know About Getting Started with Homeschool by Author Amanda Walton

I really enjoyed the voice of the narrator, she speaks in a soothing tone. The book is a really great reminder of things we might have known we could do during stressful times, but forgot over the years.

Author HarmonyHawaii

---

50 Things to Know to Manage Your Stress: Relieve The Pressure and Return The Joy To Your Life

Author Diane Whitbeck

There is so much waste in our society today. Everyone should be forced to read this book. I know I am passing it on to my family.

50 Things to Know to Downsize Your Life: How To Downsize, Organize, And Get Back to Basics

Author Lisa Rusczyk Ed. D.

Great book to get you motivated and understand why you may be losing motivation. Great for that person who wants to start getting healthy, or just for you when you need motivation while having an established workout routine.

50 Things To Know To Stick With A Workout: Motivational Tips To Start The New You Today

Author Sarah Hughes

50 THINGS TO KNOW ABOUT KNITTING

KNIT, PURL, TRICKS, & SHORTCUTS

Christina Fanelli

Cover designed by: Ivana Stamenkovic
Cover Image: https://pixabay.com/photos/wool-shop-hobby-craft-store-2742119/

CZYK Publishing Since 2011.

50 Things to Know

Lock Haven, PA
All rights reserved.
ISBN: 9798677273988

50 THINGS TO KNOW ABOUT KNITTING

BOOK DESCRIPTION

Learn two stitches and you can make just about anything! That sounds like a little too wild, but in actuality, about 90% or more of the stitches in a sweater, blanket, hat, etc. are done with one and/or two stitches.

Three of the most popular questions are: Is it easy to learn? – Yes. Are knitting patterns easy to understand? – Yes. Can I learn this if I do not know how to crochet? – Yes!

By the time you finish this book, you will know ….

1. Different types of yarn
2. Sizes of needles
3. Right-hand, Left-hand Knitting
4. Starter loops
5. Cast-on
6. Two most common stitches
7. Knit stitch
8. What to have in knitting a bag
9. Standard and Continental Style
10. Gauges
11. Knitting abbreviations and meanings
12. Start with a simple project, like a scarf or potholder
13. Different terms from different countries
14. Purl stitch
15. How to join yarns
16. How to read a pattern
17. Why use different size needles and yarn

48. How to create or adjust patterns
49. What to do with scrap yarn
50. Different stitch patterns
51. Helpful hints
52. Good for meditation
53. Group projects or time
54. Make for others (Hospital: newborn, skilled nursing, neonatal, cancer) Homeless/abuse shelters, Foster care, schools, etc.

So grab YOUR copy today. You'll be glad you did.

TABLE OF CONTENTS

DEDICATION

To my little supporting family……..Scott Congdon, Miranda Green, William Green III, and Goliath Fanelli (He's the dog you will see). I would also like to mention my deceased Grandmother, Iona Miller, who was the one that taught me the knitting we will share.

ABOUT THE AUTHOR

I started out learning to crochet then evolved into knitting. I crocheted my first child's blanket during my pregnancy and then after her birth learned from my grandmother how to knit. By the time my son was born, I could create and knit his blanket without a pattern. I have a full-time Office Management employment in a healthcare setting, so I look for mind relaxing by the end of the day. Although I find both knitting and crocheting mind beneficial, to me knitting is simpler. Life is short, relax, have fun with it, and laugh a little throughout this book! ;0)

I do can be found on Facebook, Twitter, and LinkedIn.

ProcrastiKNITing – to defer all other activities besides knitting. – AllFreeKnitting.com

INTRODUCTION

Welcome to the world of knitting. That sounds a little far and wide, but once you see how simple the two most important parts are and the options they will give you'll see that world. An introduction will be started to the basic equipment, the slight difference in left and right-hand perspectives, and then off to the hands-on learning.

The thought of knitting itself does seem to almost put fear in some people; it is actually known to have an opposite effect. Although it does affect some people differently; it is mostly known to be therapeutic, meditative, and relaxing. It works well for people that cannot sit idle, those that love arts have great imaginations, and creativity. This is due to the allowance of the mind and body to combine and create.

It is a hobby that doesn't have any specific requirements, deadlines, or skills. The ending results can be for oneself, for family, friends, pets, or even to the unknown. There is always the option of making and selling or making for people and places in need. Get started with the simple basic concept that it is all for fun and it is all for you!

1. DIFFERENT TYPES OF YARN

If you have experience in crocheting or other types of yarn artwork than you can probably skip this section or maybe even add to it. There is never too much to know when it comes to knowing the tools that you will be working with. There are different types of yarn available and there are reasons for the different types and reasons to use different types. Although at first, it will seem like a workout, it is fun. There are about 15 different types of yarn, but just like everything else, that is changing too. Yarns are different based on what they are made from, how they are made, what is the weight, and what is the ply.

Wool Yarns

There are four types of wool. Fine, medium, long, and double coated. This wool can be new/virgin wool, which means it has not been recycled or it can be Shetland wool which is Icelandic rustic wool from Scotland's islands. Wool is good for hot or cold climate and is included in fire blankets.

- Cashmere –Softest wool
- Alpaca – Super warm
- Merino – Popular chunky yarn
- Organic – Chemical free

Cotton Yarn – Light, breathable, strong and is great for warm climates

Silk Yarn –Available in reeled and spun. Is the most expensive, but is shiny, strong, and slippery.

Hemp Yarn – Natural and soft to the touch, but more often used in macramé being more fiber than cotton.

Bamboo Yarn – A natural fiber that is great for summer tops and sweaters, because it is soft and has natural antibacterial properties.

Acrylic Yarn (Man-Made) – One of the cheapest, easiest to maintain, color-fast yarns moth repellant yarns.

Novelty Yarns

There are some novel yarns, but they do tend to be more difficult to work with. They come in different textures, styles, and blends to make an assortment to choose from. Here are some of the popular styles:

- Boucle' yarn – Bumpy and loopy
- Chenille yarn –Smooth velvety like
- Thick-thin yarn – Bumpy looking
- Faux fur yarn - Looks like faux fur
- Mohair yarn – Goat hair yarn and some find it itchy
- Railroad ribbon yarn – Makes two parallel lines that look like train tracks
- Polyester yarn – Wood and cotton blend
- Ribbon yarn – Rayon, nylon, cotton yarns

When novelty yarns are taken and special colored, they become special yarns.

- Tweed yarn - The main color and fiber bit of color throughout
- Heather yarn – Many different colors or dyes in fleeces spun together
- Marled fabric rag – Numerous colors twisted together to a single strand

- Marled yarn – Two or more plies together

Yarn weight and ply

Yarn weight is the thickness of the yarn. The thickness of the yarn will be a deciding factor in the final results and the stitches per inch. The ply of yarn is how many strands are twisted together. The thickness of the yarn is displayed on the yarn label by a number, category name, and the ply based on location.

Weight	Category Name	Ply
0	Lace, Liston	UK = 1, Aus/NZ = 2
1	Super Fine, Super Fine	UK = 3 and 4, Aus/NZ = 3 and 4
2	Fine, Fine	UK = 5, Aus/NZ = 5
3	Light, Ligero	UK = DK, Aus/NZ = 8
4	Medium, Media	UK = Worsted/Aran, Aus/NZ = 10
5	Bulky, Abuttanda	UK = Bulky, Aus/NZ = 12
6	Super Bulky, Super Abuttanda	UK = Super Bulky, Aus/NZ = 16+
7	Jumbo, Jumbo	UK = Jumbo, Aus/NZ = Jumbo

The last thing I would suggest to be monitored when looking at yarn is the dye-lot number. The label will have a number for the color of the dye that was used on that skein of yarn. Make sure when purchasing more than one skein of the same color yarn for a project that you know ahead of time how many skeins you will need and that the dye-lot is the number on all of the skeins that are purchased.

2. SIZES OF NEEDLES

I find it interesting that knitting needles come in number sizes and crochet needs come in letters. Then when it is considered that the number that the USA says is the needle size, is not the same size as what the UK claims it to be, meanwhile, other countries use another size. Here is a chart of the basics and most of the internet websites have charts for the other metrics.

Metric (mm)	USA Size	UK Size	Crochet
2.00 mm	0	14	-----
2.25 mm	1	13	B
2.50 mm	1.5	-----	-----
2.75 mm	2	12	C
3.00 mm	2.5	11	-----
3.25 mm	3	10	D
3.50 mm	4	-----	E
3.75 mm	5	9	F
4.0 mm	6	8	G
4.5 mm	7	7	-----
5.0 mm	8	6	H
5.5 mm	9	5	I

6.0 mm	10	4	J
6.5 mm	10.5	3	K
7.0 mm	-----	2	-----
7.5 mm	-----	1	-----
8.0 mm	11	0	L
9.00 mm	13	00	-----
10.00 mm	15	000	-----
12-12.75 mm	17	-----	-----
15-16 mm	19	-----	-----
19 mm	35	-----	-----
20 mm	36	-----	-----
25 mm	50	-----	-----

Yes, there are other size needles. Most of the patterns that have other size needle requirements will come with adjustments and more specifications to what else you will need to accommodate the changes. The main reason I give this chart is so that you can see what is equal to what. That may sound confusing and not necessary; however, you will see in later sections why you will want the alternate sizes from this chart. (See 28)

3. RIGHT-HAND, LEFT-HAND KNITTING

Although knitting is not a sport, to some people like me it seems like it. Why do I think that it is because it takes endurance, some people are amateurs and some are professionals, you get better over time, you can become a professional, and there does come a time when many have to retire from it. However, think about all the different crafts that you will have to show in your hall of fame. Just like in sports it is mostly oriented to the majority of the people. That is the right-hand, however, there are southpaw knitters, and just like in baseball and boxing, they can do as good if not better. I am a right-hand knitter and this is written from the right-hand perspective. I did instruct my left-handed sister how to knit, but she found it easier to learn right-handed as she has done with many other activities. However, some websites are available to show you exactly how to do these same activities from the southpaw. I have a few I recommend listed at the end under "South Paw", but knitting has become such a popular sport that you will found many more and one that is perfect for you.

4. STARTER LOOPS (AKA SLIP KNOT)

If you know how to make a starter loop from crocheting, feel free to skip this section. There are different ways to make loops and there isn't a wrong way. I will show you the way that I do it and one other way that I have seen it done by others over the years. You can use either of these, any other ways that you may see in videos and pictures, or even your way. The biggest part to remember with the start out loop is to leave a tail (a piece that hangs) and that the loop is stretchable/adjustable.

Here is the step by step directions with pictures of the way that I make a starter loop:

1. Take the skein of yarn and lay it out straight with the end on the left and the skein on the right

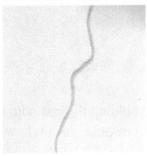

2. Take the yarn from the left side and twist it over top to make a circle

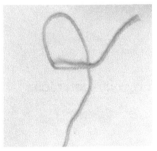

3. Holding where they cross put the end still attached to the skein through the circle (it may need to go down into the loop or from underneath and come up through)

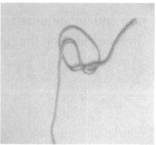

4. While holding the end with the left-hand, pull the end put through the circle with the right-hand until the string in the left-hand closes with it

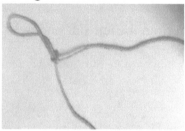

5. There is your starter loop

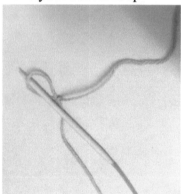

6. Put the needle in the loop and pull both ends

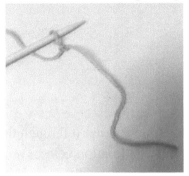

Another popular way is:

1. Take the skein of yarn and lay it out straight with the end on the left and the skein on the right

2. Take the yarn from the left side and twist it over top to make a circle

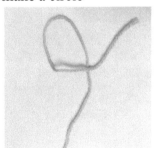

3. Move down the piece of laid out yarn and twist it over top to make a circle again

4. Take the second loop and put it through the first loop and pull until the first loop closes around the second loop. (it may need to the loop to go through from underneath and come up through)

5. There is your starter loop

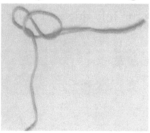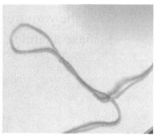

6. put the needle in the loop and pull both ends
7.

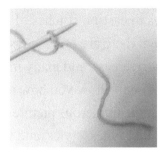

Whatever way you decide to make your loop, once it is completed, put it on the pointed end of a knitting needle and you are ready to start! Let's do this!

5. CAST-ON

There are different ways to cast-on stitches. I use the standard cast-on stitches, but there are other ways known as long tail and long tail cross overcast, and many more. They all do look a little different I will show you how to do a standard simple cast-on. Some numerous pictures and videos will show you the other types, styles, and look of cast-on stitches.

1. Put the needle that has the starter loop into the left-hand
2. Now take the needle in the right-hand and go into the left side of that loop underneath the needle that has the loop

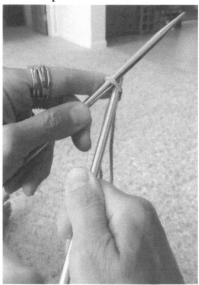

3. Take the yarn from the right side and staying underneath both needles, wrap it around the bottom needle and hold it fairly snug

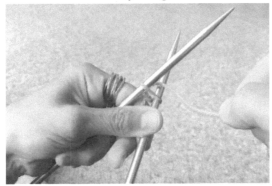

4. Slide the bottom needle towards you with the yarn wrapped around it but bring it back through the loop you went into, keeping the yarn your wrapped around pretty taught

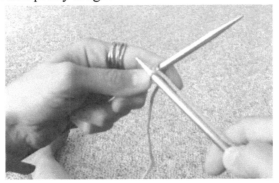

5. Pull the yarn and I mean pull the yarn towards you and pull that left-hand needle out of the way

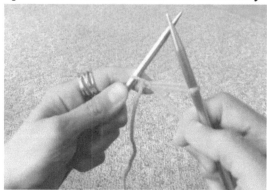

6. You now have a loop of yarn hanging on the right needle, take that loop and wrap it around the needle in your left-hand

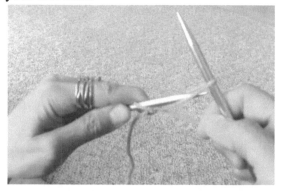

7. Now pull the yarn fairly tight to close the loop around the needle. I stress fairly tight, not tight. Leave some leeway. You now have two loops or cast-on stitches on the needle in your left-hand Repeat

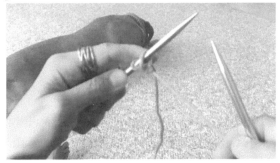

8. Do it again, take the left-hand needle, go into the new stitch on the left side underneath

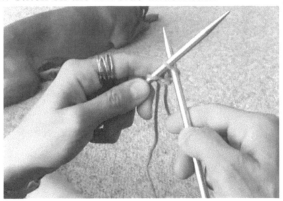

9. Wrap the yarn around the bottom left needle and pull it snug, but hold onto the yarn

10. Slide the bottom needle toward you with the yarn still wrapped around it and pull it back through where you went in.

11. Pull the yarn out so that it is stretched out long and wide. Loop in around the bottom needle again.

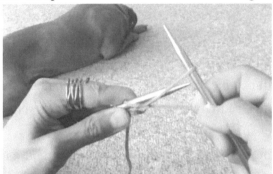

12. You now have three cast-on stitches
13. Continue this until you have the desired or required number of cast-on stitches

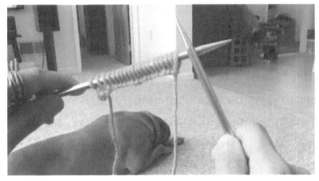

6. TWO MOST COMMON STITCHES

When you look at the different available sweater styles it is hard to perceive at this time that you will be able to make that yourself. However, if you learn the basic two stitches, you will be able to make that sweater, blanket, scarf, or anything else that you can find a pattern for. Now it seems unbelievable, but it is possible.

There are basically two stitches in knitting. Now you can use either one of these stitches and make anything, both of these stitches and make things, and as you will later see you can make some slight changes on how you use these stitches and make things look different.

I am first going to teach you the knit stitch. We will then cover a couple of subjects before we go onto the purl stitch. I do this for a reason. Many times when beginners try to learn both stitches in the beginning they confuse the two of them and it is harder to get "un"confused. Therefore, I always teach knit stitch, have you work with it for a while doing a few things, and then later teach you the purl stitch when we know that you have the knit stitch in your head. Let's begin.

7. KNIT STITCH

Now that you have all the desired number of the stitches that you want or need cast onto a needle we will learn to do a knit stitch. It is a basic simple step that you already know how to do! I know you thinking you don't, but if you completed the cast-on….you do! So here we go.

1. Put the needle with the stitches on it in your left-hand with the point aiming to the right

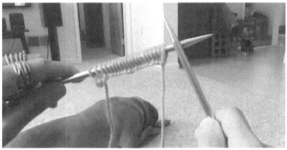

2. Go into the stitch that is closest to the tip of the needle, on the left side just like you did before when you were casting on

3. Wrap the yarn around just like you did to cast-on

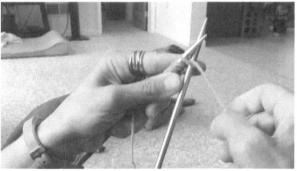

4. Pull the yarn back through, just like when you did the cast-on

5. However, instead of stretching out the yarn to put on the left-hand needle, you're going to slide the stitch that you went into off of the left needle

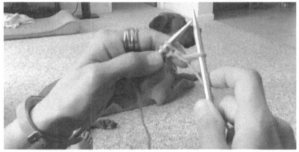

6. You will now have one stitch on the right needle and your remaining stitches on the left needle
7. Repeat. Go into the next stitch on the left need with the right needle, underneath from the left side

8. Wrap the yarn around the bottom needle

9. Pull it back through

10. Slide the stitch you went through off of the left needle.

11. You now have two stitches on the right needle
12. Continue this until you no longer have stitches on the left needle, when you complete the last stitch, you finished your first row!

13. When all the stitches are on the right needle, swap the needles around so that all the stitches are back in the left-hand and the right-hand needle is empty again.

14. After a few rows, it will look like below

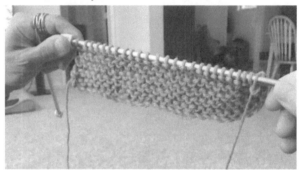

You are now knitting! I suggest that you continue to do the knit stitch for at least a couple of hours before you proceed. I do not mean that you have to knit for a couple of hours straight. Take a break here and there. See if you understand and have the swing of it. Do it for 20 minutes today and then again tomorrow or the next day for 10 minutes. If you take a day off do you need to look at the directions again? If not, you are set to move on to learn the purl stitch. However, I do have a few informational things to cover while you practice the knit stitch. I also suggest that you do a complete row (all the stitches are on one needle) before you stop. Stopping in the middle of the needle of stitches on a row is sometimes difficult to decide which needle goes in which hand when it's picked back up. This can cause you to restart in the wrong direction if the needles are not in the correct hands.

8. KNITTING BAG

I know that sounds a little strange to be talking about already, but it is something that you will eventually want to have. That is because many things are used in knitting. Some of them are necessary, but most of them are just to make things easier now and in the future. Therefore, a knitting bag is just where to keep all of your current projects and supplies. I have found that bags that are donated to you at benefits work great. They are usually given to you to gather things at the benefit, so gather your knitting supplies in it.

Of course, the first thing to think about having in the knitting bag is the yarn and the needles that will be used to complete your project. But here are a few other things that I would suggest that you keep your knitting bag. They are not essential but do come in handy when working right along on a sweater, hat, or any other knitting project.

I have found that most of my supplies are small and it is easier to keep them all in a smaller bag. Here are some of the items that I suggest that you include in your kitting bag in a smaller bag: Scissors, tape measures, markers, safety pins, stitch holders, sticky notes, pens, yarn needles, a gauge ruler, scrap yarn and more. I know that sounds like a lot of little things to have in a bag. I go to the school supplies section and acquire a pencil pouch with a zipper or a zip-lock storage bag and use them to store all of these items. I am sure you know what the small scissors and tape measure/rule are for, but do you know what a marker or the post-it notes are for? Now, none of this is mandatory, just things that I have found useful over the years and why. Anything that is no longer used that can hold small items in them is great for these bags, sometimes I have found that the package that kids games or pieces for their games come in are perfect storages for safety pins, markers, etc.

- Markers and safety pins are all pretty much used for the same thing. They are all used to help you keep track of certain locations. Example: You have knitted to a point and you will need to put a button on a sweater. The pattern will tell you to knit so many stitches and put a marker. This marker can be a safety pin, a piece of old yarn that is knotted or even purchased circles that will go around the needle. These are very helpful later in the pattern. They can mark where to change from knit to purl and vice versa and many other pattern changes.

- Sticky notes and pens may seem a little strange, but I have found them to be helpful in numerous ways. When you are working on a pattern, you can use the edge of the sticky note to mark the last completed line of the pattern when you are ready to put it down. The can be used to keep track of counts for you. Some patterns will tell you to do "X" amount of rows before you do the next step. The old fashioned Tally Marks can be used to track the number of rows you have completed and then you have the freedom to stop whenever you want. I have also found them to be handy when I am knitting something that has to have a duplicate for the same reason. I like my sweaters long, so I make them longer than the pattern says Tally marks allow me to put the same amount of extra rows where necessary.

- A gauge ruler can come in handy when you need to know the size of what needles are in your bag. They also help to decide what size is the alternate needle. For example, if you are working with a size 1 knitting needle and you need a crochet hook, this ruler will show you a size "B" crochet hook is the same size as a size "1" knitting needle. Many of them have a small ruler along with the size of them in inches, millimeters, and centimeters for measurements.

- Stitch holders and end caps. Stitch holders are used like huge safety pins. These are used often in sweater patterns. They are used to hold stitches for use later. If you are making a sweater you may have to put the stitches for the neck on a stitch holder while you complete the shoulders on each side. End caps are handy if you have a lot of stitches on the needles or if you are using cable needles (see 21). They come in assorted sizes and are rubbery. These are placed on the ends of the needles and keep the stitches on the needles when you put it down or in your bag.

- An old skein of yarn can be used for a lot of the things that have been mentioned above and more. If you find that you have a little ball of yarn leftover, keep in it your knitting bag near your scissors. Take and cut about 2" strips and make a knot close to the ends and you have some markers for when the pattern requests it. Scrap yarn works out great when an exact stitch must be marked. You can cut a piece of the yarn, slip it through the stitch and knot it. Now that stitch is not going to come undone and it is marked. You can pick up that stitch and just cut the marker yarn off. A long string of old yarn can also be used instead of a stitch holder. Take a long piece of the old yarn and string it through the eye of the yarn needle. Now slip the needle through each stitch that needs to be used later and then pull the old yarn through. Once you have all the stitches that need to be on the holder, tie a knot with the two ends and you have a very mobile, flexible stitch holder. I say mobile holder because the yarn makes the stitches that are being held easier to move and less apt to catch on other stitches.

Old Yarn

Stitch Holder and Needle Caps

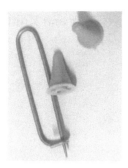

Sticky Notes and Pen

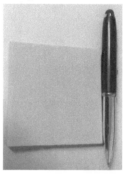

Scissors, Measuring tape, Needle Gauge

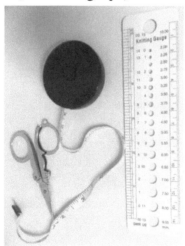

Crochet Hook and Knitting Needle

Safety Pins

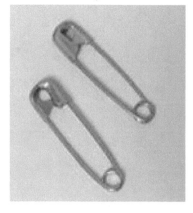

Yarn Makers and Plastic Marker

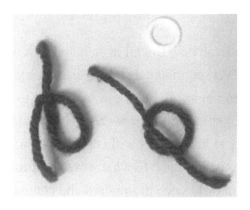

Here is a picture of all of them   A
  school supplies bag to keep them all in.

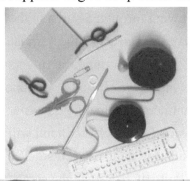

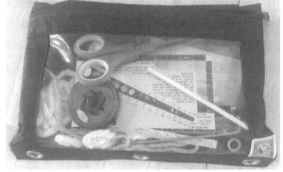

9. STANDARD AND CONTINENTAL STYLE

I showed you how to knit in standard (AKA English) style, however, continental style is also a very popular way to knit. I do not use it, but it can be helpful to know how to do it and for some people it is easier. As I said, there is no correct way to knit, things will come to you naturally over time and you will adjust to what works best for you.

The main difference in standard and continental knitting is the way that the yarn is held. When the knitting is done standard (the way I do it) the skein of yarn is on the right side for yarn overs. The right-hand moves the yarn around the needle that went through a stitch in the needle of the left-hand. In continental style, the yarn is on the left side and the yarn is wrapped around the fingers on the left-hand for it to do the yarn over. If you have done crocheting before, the Continental style may be easier for you. The yarn is on the side for whichever hand will wrap the yarn around, right side for standard, left side for continental. All the rest of the knit stitch is done the same, no matter which style you are doing. Any pictures you see throughout are standard style, but there is a link at the end that shows continental style if you would like to see the difference.

10. GAUGES

A gauge is a sample or estimate. It is used to give you an idea of the size you are creating. What I mean by this is if you have two yarns that are a weight of 2 and 4 and knit a gauge of 25 stitches (the usually suggested quantity) with the same size needle, they are going to come out different measurements. The one that uses the weight yarn size 2 is going to be smaller in width and length compared to the one that is the weight of 4. The same will happen if you use the same size yarn, but two different needle sizes. A size 5 needle with a 4 weight yarn is going to be smaller than a gauge with a size 10 needle with a 4 weight yarn. These result for the same reasons, because of the difference in the thickness of the yarn and/or the difference in the thickness (circumference) of the needle.

The main point behind doing a gauge is to decide how many stitches you need to get a specific measurement based on the yarn weight and the needle size. You will see that most patterns will give you the size of the needle and the weight of the yarn to use, but I still suggest you do a gauge. This is because different people knit at different levels of tightness and that will make the 25 stitch gauge bigger or smaller. Then you may have to adjust the needle size to make it the correct measurement. When I do a recommended gauge, I usually have to go a needle size smaller than suggested. That is because I tend to be taut with my yarn. I suggest you do a gauge before starting any big project that is based on a measurement (to be worn), mainly so that it comes out to the desired measurements or if you are going to adjust the yarns. So for example the pattern is for a sweater, do a gauge with the desired yarn to see if the measurement matches the pattern. If you decide to use a smaller or larger weight yarn, again, do a gauge to see that the measurement will be correct.

To do a gauge, cast-on 25 stitches with the suggested needle and yarn. Knit across to the end and then switch the hands the needles are in and repeat. Do 25 knit rows and then take a measurement. In this case, the gauge should measure 5 x 5 if the yarn and needles are correct. If not, then some adjustments are necessary. We will go into more detail, differences, and how to adjust in more detail when we start patterns. (See 16). Two gauges are below of 25 stitches. They show how much difference there can be in width when the needles are the same, but the stitches change. Both of the colors are done with the same size needle and weight of yarn continuously, but as you can see the types of stitches changes how wide the measurement will be. That is why I ways suggest a gauge based on the pattern.

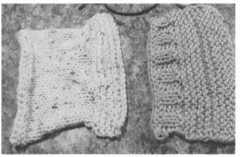

11. KNITTING ABBREVIATIONS AND MEANINGS

When reading a pattern it sometimes scares people. There are a lot of abbreviations that are used in knitting to shorten a pattern. Imagine if you were making a blanket for a king-size bed and it told you to do the same row from beginning to end. It would be a book with the same direction line, over and over again probably 5000+times. The marks *……* is used around a section when it is to be repeated is very common. Here is a list of some of the other most common. Some websites will give a free printout of "all of them". I say "All of them" because I still find new ones that I add to my list. Some will look a little foreign right now, but you will know soon.

Abbreviation	Meaning
bo	bind off
co	cast-on
dec	decrease
dpn	double-pointed needles
inc	increase
k	knit
k2tog	knit 2 stitches together, makes a right-leaning decrease
m	marker
M1	Make one
p	purl

pat	pattern
pm	place a marker
p2tog	purl 2 stitches together, makes a left-leaning decrease
rem	remaining
rep	repeat
rnd	round
sl	slip
ssk	slip 2 stitches knitwise. Will make a left-leaning
ssp	slip 2 stitches purlwise. Will make a left-leaning
St st	Stockinette stitch – Knit row, purl next, knit row, purl row, repeat
tog	together
ws	wrong side
yo	yarn over

12 START WITH A SIMPLE PROJECT

I always suggest that you start with a simple project for your first attempt. In my class, I suggest they try a scarf. That is because it is good to teach you the knit stitch with a lot of practice stitches and then show you the purl stitch for a lot of stitches. Your first project is going to be messy. You are going to have holes, gaps, lost and added stitches, etc. This is normal. You are learning how tight you like to hold your yarn so it may start at 5 inches and then be 6 inches because you start to hold the yarn looser and not make your stitches so tight. Remember, this is your first project. It's like riding a bike, you are wobbly, falling, hitting all kinds of bumps, but you won't eventually…..and you'll have the hang of it soon.

After doing both of the stitches for a while, you can then continue one or both of them until you get the scarf to the length that you want. However, if you don't want a scarf and know that you understand both of the stitches and can remember the difference in the two, bind it off (I'll show you later) and you have a potholder. If it is too messy looking, slide the needle that has all the stitches on it out so all the stitches fall off it and pull that string. You can start all over.

13. DIFFERENT TERMS FROM DIFFERENT COUNTRIES

You will recall in the beginning the yarn and the needles did come with alternate language translations. That is because they are very common and very different terms or verbiage that is used in knitting. Do not be afraid when you see a word in a pattern that you do not know what it means. Like I said above, I am still adding abbreviations and I still look on the internet for definitions and videos of what something means. I have found over the years that I knew that just never heard it called that. A common example is CO or Cast Off, which is the same as BO or Bind off.

14. PURL STITCH

I think that you are ready to learn the other stitch, the purl. It is similar to the knit stitch, but with a couple of modifications.

1. Put the needle with the stitches on it in your left-hand with the point aiming to the right, with the yarn on the front side of the needle in your left-hand

2. Go into the stitch that is closest to the tip of the needle, on the **right** side and go underneath, just like you did before when you were knitting

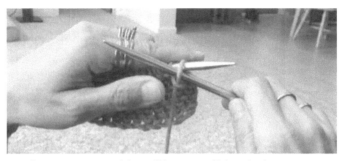

3. Wrap the yarn around just like you did to knit

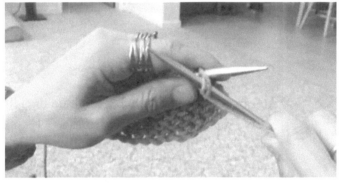

4. Pull the yarn back through, just like when you did to knit

5. Slide the stitch that you went into off of the left needle, just like the knit stitch

6. You will now have one stitch on the right needle and your remaining stitched on the left needle – you did a purl stitch

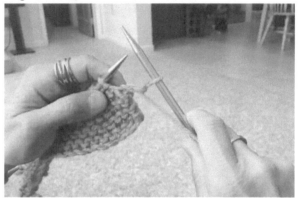

7. Repeat. Go into the next stitch on the left need with the right needle and the yarn in front, underneath from the right side

8. Wrap the yarn around the bottom needle

9. Pull it back through

10. Slide the stitch you went through off of the left needle.

11. You now have two stitches on the right needle
12. Continue this until you no longer have stitches on the left needle, when you complete the last stitch, you finished your first purl row!
13. When all the stitches are on the right needle, swap the needles around so that all the stitches are back in the left-hand and the right-hand needle is empty again and put the yarn in the front again
14. Repeat

Again, I recommend that you do this for a while to get the swing of the change. However many rows or amount of time you spent in the knitting to get this swing of it, is probably what you will need for the purl stitch too. Here is a way to remember the differences between the two once you have the swing of them. This might sound a little corny, but this is how I remember it. I again suggest that you do a complete row (all the stitches are on one needle) before you stop.

K = Knit	**P** = Purl
L = Left	**R** = Right.

K is before **P** in the alphabet

L comes before **R** in the alphabet

Knit goes into the stitch on the **L**eft side

Purl goes into the stick on the **R**ight side

So basically when doing knit go in on the left of the stitch on the left needle and when doing purl go in on the right of the stitch of the stitch on the left needle. Take your time and after you get the swing of the purl stitch and know that you can remember the difference, you are set to start picking patterns and making what you want.

15. HOW TO JOIN YARNS

When you knit any project of size or color you will come across a time when you will have to join yarns. This can be done with a simple basic knot, however, some are easier to hide in the garment or that are not a knot at all. I am going to show you a double know and a Russian join, but there are much more available online so find what you like. I like the first one, a double knot.

The one I use is two knots and slide (double knot)

1. Put the two strings of yarn next to each other horizontally with ends going opposite directions

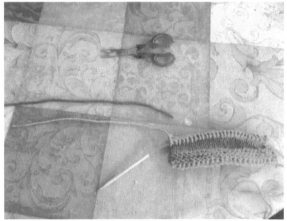

2. Take the open end and wrap it around the string and make a loop

3. Take the string and come up through the loop (making a snug knot around the string)

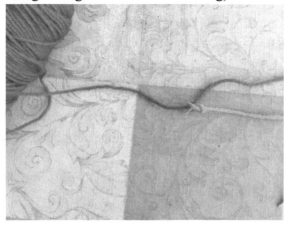

4. Now do the same at the other end

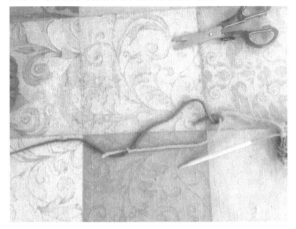

5. When both knots are complete slowly pull both strings of yarn and the knots will slowly approach each other

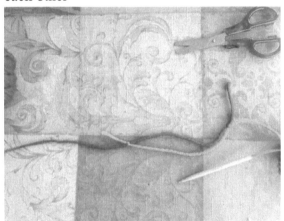

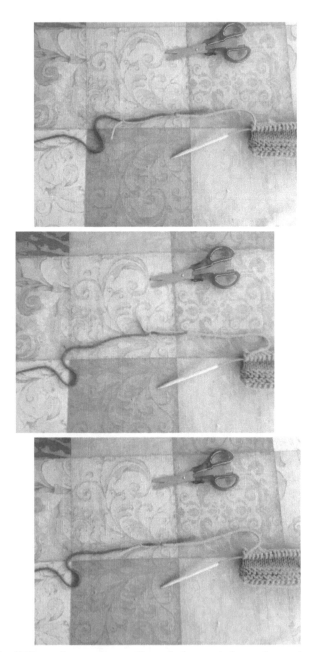

6. When they meet pull each knot tight and cut the
   knot ends off

7. You are good to go!

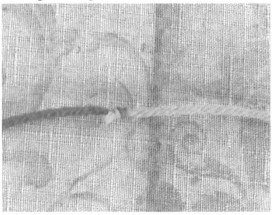

Another common join is called a Russian join
1. Put the two strings of yarn next to each other horizontally with ends going opposite directions

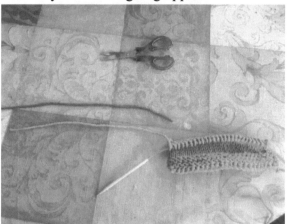

2. Untwist the yarn on each skein for about 3 inches or more, keeping the skeins separated

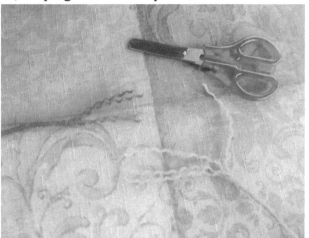

3. Once you have each skein yarn untwisted you will find separate strings within (if its 4ply, 4 strands; if it's 3ply, 3 strands; etc.)

4. Now take a strand from the left skein and twist it with a strand from right skein

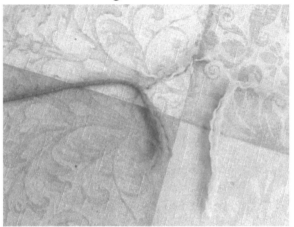

5. Repeat until all strands on left skein are twisted with strands from right skein (if its 4ply, 4 strands; if it's 3ply, 3 strands; etc.)

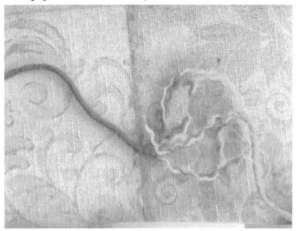

6. Now twist the combined strands together until the end of the original skein (cut off skein or end of the prior skein)

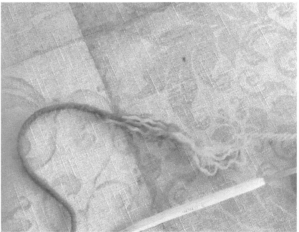

7. You are good to go!

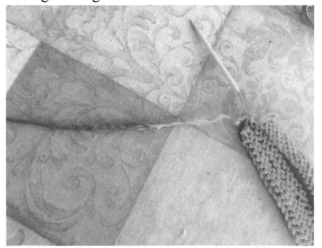

16. HOW TO READ A PATTERN

I am not going to go into a lot of detail here. Mainly because there isn't a mandatory set way for patterns to be written so you will always see something new in a pattern. However, most of the time you will see that it is set up in roughly the following format with the following basic information.

1. Supplies needed
2. Yarn colors in the picture
3. Size options (if clothing)
4. Gauge
5. Notes
6. There will be notes throughout

You will be given the suggested gauge to try. This is a number of stitches to cast-on and a number of rows to complete with the suggested needle size. This is to give you an idea of the suggested needle size that will give you the correct measurements. So if it says to do 10 stitches/14 rows = 4" in SS, that means to take the suggested needle, cast-on 10 stitches and do stockinet stitch (knit a row, purl a row) for 14 rows and see if it measures a perfect square of 4" inches wide by 4" length. If it's bigger than 4 x 4 go to a smaller needle, if smaller than 4 x 4 go to a larger needle. Once you know the size of the needle you need, go ahead and cast-on and start your project.

What you will see from here depends on what you are making. The supplies will be mostly the same, maybe additional needles needed for areas in the pattern. Yarn colors, of course, are up to you, you can change them however you want. Size options may or may not be present. If it's a blanket or scarf maybe not, but if it's a sweater or slipper, yes. They tend to be put in this type of format: Chest 35(39, 43, 46, 50, 53, 57). That means that you want to make one of these chest sizes, follow the quantity inside the parenthesis to see how many you need. Example: I want to make a chest size 39 sweater, so the number of needed stitches section says CO 44 (48, 52, 56, 60, 64, 68) sts. Using the format you would cast-on 48 stitches.

There will be notes throughout as mentioned because as you go through a pattern say for a sweater, it will tell you to keep checking your measurements, to change patterns, bind off (we will get to it), etc. Therefore, it is important when starting a project to read the whole pattern. Sweaters, socks, slippers, gloves, etc. tend to be sectional. Make a piece, bind it off, put it aside, do the next piece. Once all the pieces are done, sew them together.

17. WHY USE DIFFERENT SIZE NEEDLES AND YARN

As you may have figured out from the description in the gauges, using different size needles makes for different size garments. When you get to the point of being able to create your projects keep in mind the differences in yarns and needles. If the yarn is thicker, there will be fewer stitches per inch and if the needle is thicker, there will be fewer stitches per inch. It goes the same for thinner yarn and smaller needles you will need to increase the number of stitches per inch. There are times when you will want to exchange your needles. For example, on a sweater, a pattern may be suggested to start with a size 5 needle for the first 10 rows and then change to a size 7 needle for the remaining. This is to make the bottom of a sweater tighter and then the body a little larger. Make sure if you are adjusting the 5 to a 4 needle, that you also adjust the 7 to a 6 needle too.

18. HOW TO MAKE A FLAT PATTERN

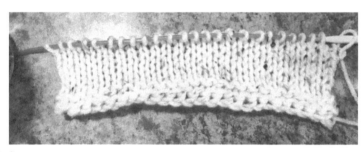

Knit

Purl

Now that you know how to do both a knit and a purl stitch I'm going to point out something to you. When you look at sweaters, there is a flat like a pattern. So far, what you have done doesn't show or create this. That is because you are repeating the same stitch. In the beginning, we were doing a knit stitch, then exchanging the hands the needles are in and doing a knit stitch again. Later we did a purl stitch then exchanged the hands that the needles are in and do a purl again. To make a flat pattern you need to do one stitch, then exchange hands and do the other, opposite. This is called stockinette (St st). Example: Knit a row, exchange the needles, and then do a purl row, exchange the needles and do a knit row, repeat a few times. Now, look at each side. One side is flat and the other side is raised. A little secret here is the flat side is the knit, the raised side is the purl. So if you put down the knitting and pick it back up, put the needle with the stitches on it in the left-hand and look at the pattern. If it's flat, then knit. If the pattern is raised, then purl.

19. STITCH TYPES TO CREATE

When you decide that you are comfortable with both stitches, I would suggest that you make something that doesn't need a pattern, a scarf, blanket, potholder, etc. I suggest this so that you can get an idea of the different yarns, stitches, and sizes before you try to read patterns. I would probably suggest potholders because they are small and you could try a couple of things. I would suggest 4 weight yarn, size 8 or bigger needle, and do a gauge of 20 stitches, 20 rows. This will tell you how many stitches for you in an inch. Now you can decide how big you want your potholder. We will do a 6 x 6. So if you go through with the gauge and find that 5 stitches are an inch then to make a 6 x 6 you will need 30 cast-on stitches and about 30 rows. Another suggestion is that you try doing 6 rows of purl, then a row of knit, then a row of purl, then a row of knit, then a row of purl (stockinette stitch) until you get to 5 inches. This is to show you that a stockinette stitch, will give you flat on one side and puffy on the other. When you get the five inches, do the remaining rows in all knit rows. This will a flat look on one side and a puffy look on the other, with the trim the same on both sides. Once you have completed the 30 rows or got the 6 inches in the rows, a bind of should be done. See the next section, for how to do a bind off.

20. BIND OFF

The term bind of explains itself. What you are going to do, is close (bind) off the stitches. There are different ways to bind off stitches. I will explain and show you the way I do it. It is a standard bind off. At first, it is going to seem like you are doing a stitch, which you are, but it's the last part that changes. Here we go.

1. It does not matter if it is a knit or purl stitch. Do two of the stitches

2. Go into the left side of the first stitch and pull it over top of the first stitch

3. Slide it off the needle

4. Do the next stitch (knit or purl) normal

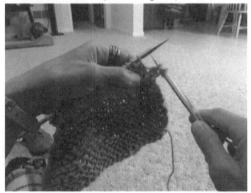

5. Repeat steps 2-4. Take the prior stitch and pull it up and over the recent stitch
6. Slide it off the needle

7. Repeat to the end

8. Stretch the last stitch out and cut the yarn and feed it back through the stitch

21. BLANKETS – BLOCKS, STRIPS, CABLE NEEDLES, ETC.

Now that you know how to do knit and purl we will look at blankets. There are different options available for blankets. There are patterns available for special designs such as seed stitch, Herringbone, and many others; however, we are going to work with what we know at this point. You should know though that you are at the point where you can do just about any knitting design. You may need to watch YouTube videos and pause for some steps, but you are at the point where you can do it. Blankets can be done in a few different simple ways. Blocks, strips, and cable needles. So we will look at each of them and you can decide what you want to try first. There are links for each of these styles in the reference section.

The blocks pattern, you have already done. When you did the potholder, you did a block. For the blanket pick the size of the block that you want and find your needle and yarn weight to use and make the blocks. You can make as many blocks as you want and then put them together to make a blanket. These blocks can put together using border knitting (We do it in section 23) or be sewn together (We do it in section 33). This is a common use for leftover yarns that are then sewn or knitted together with a neutral color.

Another way to make a blanket is to make long or short strips. If they are long strips they are usually about 12-14 inches wide and then the desired length. It only takes three of these to be wide enough for a twin size bed but can take 10 or more for a king-size bed depending on if an overhang is desired. Once all of the desired lengths are bound off lay them next to each other and sew them together. (see section 20)

We have not seen any cable needles yet, but they are my favorite. They are great for blankets. They are knitting needles on each end, but with a cable line connecting them. The main point of them is to be able to put more stitches on them than you can with just two needles. This is because the needles themselves can hold the same amount of stitches as standard needles, but the cable can also hold stitches. The number of stitches it can hold depends on the length of the cable. They come in many different lengths.

Most of mine are 24" cables, but I have seen some that are 48" and 64". This would make it so that you could put the whole width of the blanket on the needles and continue to knit and purl across in any desired pattern, again using the markers to show you when to make the change in a pattern. I use these for just about all of my projects even a potholder. This is because I take my knitting all over the place to work on. So if I am on a bus trip, I can work with the cabled needles in a small space. I can work on a project and they will not be sticking out past my allotted space or poking the window or person sitting next to me.

22. HOW TO HIDE THE ENDS

When you first start knitting or just finish a project you will have a string hanging. There are many different ways to hide the strings. You may find others that you like better, but I weave them into the existing stitches for better blending.

1. Take the needle and weave it through some exiting stitches, I would go through at least four

2. Thread the end of the yarn through the eye of the needle

3. Pull the needle through the pattern and remove the needle

4. Pull the end excessively past the pattern and cut it off

5. Let the pattern fall back naturally

23. HOW TO PICK UP STITCHES

Here is how to do a border when you complete a blanket or any project that you want to put a border, collar, cuff, etc. around the edge. This is more for decoration and can add an inch or two to the measurements all the way around. If you know how to crochet and would like to crochet a border, skip this section and go to section 24 b. I am sure there are several different ways to pick up stitches that you can find on the internet, but here is a simple one that I have used over the years.

1. Put the crochet hook under the top row, in between two stitches

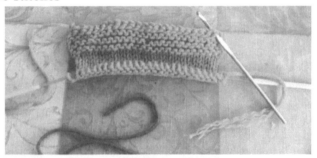

2. Yarn over the crochet hook with an excess tail

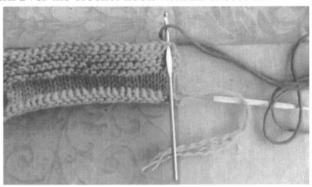

3. Pull the yarn over through where you went in, but do not pull through the excess tail

4. Go in under the next top row, in between two stitches

5. Yarn over the crochet

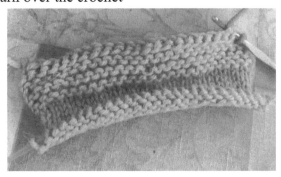

6. Pull the yarn over through where you went in

7. Repeat

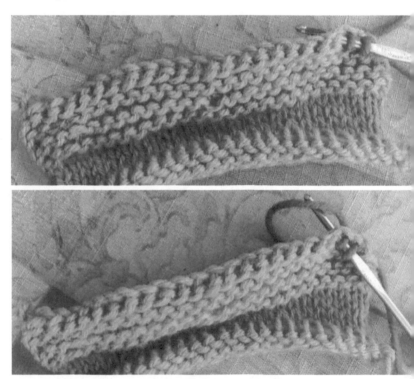

8. Continue with 5-8 until you get all the stitches you want to have the border

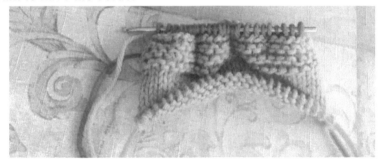

9. Slip the stitches from the crochet hook to a knitting needle slowly

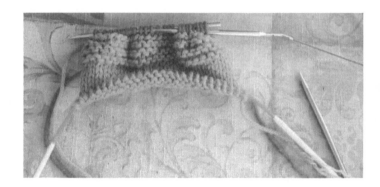

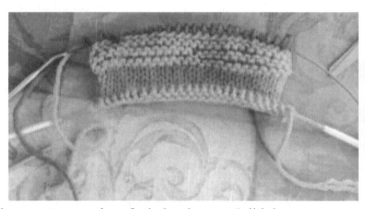

Now there were not a lot of stitches here so I did them all at once, but you may have to move the stitches to the knitting needle as you go along. Therefore, I suggest that you have a crochet hook like the one here. It has a smooth end and the entire crochet hook is the same circumference. I have some that have a larger handle on them to prevent stitches from sliding off and some have decorations that make them difficult to slide stitches over. They are more for ergonomics and stability of stitches on knitting projects.

Depending on the size of the project and the length of the cable, you can continue and go around the whole border to pick up stitches or just do one side at a time. See section 26 for a few different types of boarders.

24. INCREASE STITCHES

I am going to explain how to do one type of increase stitches. There are numerous other ways to do these, but these are the ones that I have found the easiest. To do an increase in stitches you will go into the back and the front of the stitch on the needle. Which part to go into first depends on if it is a knit or a purl stitch that you are going into. We are going to do a knit stitch, which is easier.

1. Go into the back first

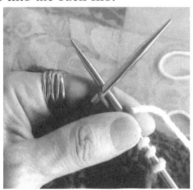

2. Do the yarn over

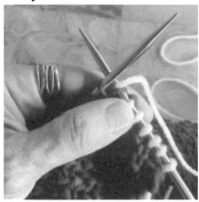

3. WITHOUT slipping it off the needle

4. Go into the front part of the stitch on the needle

5. Yarn over

6. Slide it off

7. You will have increased it from one stitch to two stitches

If it is a purl you are going into do the same but go into the front first. You will be able to tell based on the appearance. I find it easier to do the increase on a knit side.

25. DECREASE STITCHES

To decrease the stitches a pattern may suggest for you to bind them off. I do not like to do bind-offs in some areas. A couple of areas specifically are the sleeve and neck areas. The choice is yours, but I think to bind off make it more difficult to pick up stitches in a neat looking manner, it looks more geometric to me and sometimes leaves small holes that only I see. I do the k2tog or p2tog. It will still decrease the number of stitches and it makes it blend more in my opinion. The pictures below are k2tog, but it is done the same for p2tog.

1. Go into two stitches at the same time

2. Yarn over

3. Slip both stitches back through

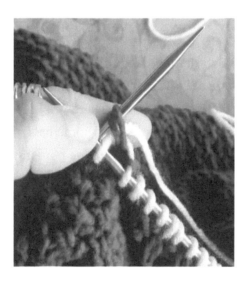

4. Slide off the needle

26. BORDER STYLE AND NEEDLE SIZE

There are different types of borders that you can create. Some styles look better on blankets, others look better on slippers and scarfs. If you are going by a pattern, there probably is a border included. However, if you are making your own there are different types to choose from. Here are a couple of patterns that I use. There is a link in the references for different styles and some have the directions.

    a. To knit a straight edge border, it is just like standard knitting. The stitches that you picked up on the cable needle will be used just like before. You can do any pattern you want such as all knit, a knit row then a purl row (so it is flat on one side and raised on the other) or knit two, purl two so it is more textured. If it is a large project like a blanket, I suggest that you put a marker when you pick up the last stitch so that you know where the end is to make an even number of rows. Again, it is up to you on what pattern you use and how many rows you do.

b. Crocheted borders are often used to accentuate. You can, of course, go around the border and pick up every other stitch and do a standard crochet stitch of your choice. I suggest that you put a marker where you start so that you know where the end is to make an even number of rows. You can do the entire border in whichever crochet stitch you want and for however many rows you want. In the end, you will know that it is the same size, stitch, and number of rows all the way around.

27. HAT

There are different ways that hats can be knitted. They can be completed with standard knitting and then sewn together, they can be done with a cable needle to a point and then split and then a small section sewn together or they can be done with double-pointed needles and not need to be sewn together. There are patterns available for all of these. However, I do want to point out that at this point doing standard knitting or cable needle would be the easiest for you if you are looking for patterns. Here is a briefing on double-pointed needles. The hat is usually suggested to be done on cable needles until a point, then change to double pointed needles. There is a link in the references to give you pictures and a great description of how to do a complete hat with double-pointed needles.

1. Count out how many stitches you have left on the needles and divide it by 4
2. Slip that number of stitches onto the four separate needles making sure that the stitch that has the skein attached is on the right end of a needle. (You may want to put rubber stoppers on the ends of the needles not in use to prevent them from sliding off if you have a lot of stitches on them)
3. Take the fifth needle and looking at the needle where the skein of yarn is, start the pattern until you get to the last stitch on that needle
4. Move to the next needle on the right, putting it in your left-hand and using the needle all the stitches

were knitted from using it as the needle in your right-hand to do the stitches

5. Repeat step 4
6. Most likely the pattern will be telling you to k2tog, watch that this is done throughout all the needles, and remove a needle as needed.

If you do the standard knitting you will just sew the sides together and the decrease in the stitches will make the hat round off on the top. However, using the cable or the double point needles will decrease, but I have a suggestion. When you get to the last row of decrease, pull out the yarn and leave a long string and cut it. Take this string that is still attached and put it through a yarn needle. Put that needle through each stitch on the knitting needle and pull. This will close the hole at the top. If you used the five needles you should be done, knot it, and weave the end into the hat. If you used the cable needle you have a small section to sew together, so continue with that long strand and sew the two sides together. Once it is closed, knot it, and weave it in.

Here is an assortment of hats I have made with my favorite model that you may have seen in the background of some of my other snapshots.

28. GLOVE VS MITTEN

I am not going to go into a lot of details about gloves and mittens. If you are giving these a thought you are doing very well. However, I would suggest that if you are willing to try these that you do the mitten first and find one of the patterns that have the glove done in half and then sewn together. The thumb is the most difficult part and it does look best when completed with the multiple double-pointed needles. With that said, the fingers to a mitten are usually done with double-pointed needles. I have seen patterns that do the fingers in length instead of width or sewn on later.

29. BABY OUTFITS

If you decide that you would like to try making a sweater, I would suggest you make one for a baby first. This is because sweaters can be time-consuming and when it is one of your first projects I suggest you get some practice with quick finishes before you start long projects like adult sweaters and Afghans. There is a large selection of the different patterns for baby outfits and there are other simple practice starters like slippers, hats, and your first sweater in any style.

30. DIFFERENT NEEDLE SIZES FOR SWEATER CUFF AND EDGES

Some patterns will tell you that you will need two different size needles. This is because you may be using the same amount of stitches, but you need to decrease or increase the size. An example of this is when you are making the arm of a sweater. Some patterns will have you start with the smaller needle and then increase the size of the needle and increase the number of stitches (in front and back o fa stitch). This is to start at the wrist and slowly make the sleeve get bigger around for the elbow and armpit. Therefore, you will start with the smaller needle for the wrist and then change to the larger needle for the arm. Other patterns will do exactly the opposite, start with the larger number of stitches for the shoulder and then have you decrease the quantity of stitches (K2tog) to the wrist. These changes in needles sizes may also be the case for edges on blankets, potholders, bags, etc.

31. TRANSITIONING MEASUREMENTS FOR YARN LENGTH DESCRIPTION

As you progress in knitting and looking at patterns in different locations, you will find that not all of them are in the same format. Some patterns will be in Inches, some will be in Millimeters, some will be in Centimeters, etc. You may remember seeing the mm in the needles sizes. There are charts available to show what measurement equals what on the internet. However, I tend to just Google it. So, I work in Inches and the pattern comes in

Millimeters. I will Google Millimeters to Inches and put the differences on my sticky note on the pattern.

32. TRANSITIONING MEASUREMENTS FOR YARN WEIGHT

Yarn comes in different weights and you may need to make adjustments based on patterns. You may also find this when it comes to measurements in yarns. The yarn label or pattern may list yards (yds) and/or meters (m). Make sure you are looking at the right measurement type. Some patterns and yarns are labeled in grams (g). These patterns or yarns that are listed by grams are regarding the weights (thickness) of the yarn, so be careful when reading charts and labels. You may have to do calculations to know how much yarn in the number of meters is and in yards. There are calculators available on Google that will let you just enter in the quantities of meters and it will instantly give you the results of yards and vice versa.

33. STITCH HOLDERS OR STRING OF YARN MARKER

As mentioned in section 8, there is a stitch holder. It is the one that looks like an oversized safety pin that is used to hold stitches that will be used later. So for example when you are at the area on the sweater where a neck will be, knit across the shoulder and then place the suggested number of stitches on the stitch holder. This is done by opening the large safety pin and you slip the stitch from the knitting needle to the stitch holder. Once you have the suggested quantity, close the stitch holder like you do a safety pin and knit the other shoulder. Now the same procedure would be done for placing the stitches on a string of yarn, except that you thread the knitting needle with the yarn. When you put the needle through a stitch and the yarn goes through it, slide it off the knitting needle. Once you have all of the suggested stitches on the piece of yarn, remove the needle and tie the ends in a knot. Either of these methods can be used, but I prefer the string of yarn for two reasons. One, when I go to take the stitches back off the stitch holder, there is only one direction that they can come off, and sometimes that is the wrong end to start the pattern on. The other reason I like the string of yarn is that it is more flexible so I can make the string of yarn as long as I want so I don't need an assortment of stitch holders, numerous ones to hold many stitches, and it can hang anyway I want it. This makes it easier to see what I am doing and not worry about the ends of the stitch holder getting caught in my pattern.

Here are pictures of how to do the two different stitch holders. This is with the stitch holder that looks like a large safety pin.

The next pictures are using a string of yarn. I did this removing the stitches from the stitch holder instead of a knitting needle, but everything would be done the same. I like the yarn better. It's more flexible and I can decide which end I start from when I am going to be picking the stitches back up.

34. SEW PIECES TOGETHER

There are numerous ways to sew pieces together like putting the arm on a sweater or strips of a blanket. I will show you step-by-step the way that I find easiest and it looks neat. However, the internet has numerous different ways to do it so you can always look and see if there is one that you find easier to follow.

1. Lie the two pieces next to each other spread out as much as possible

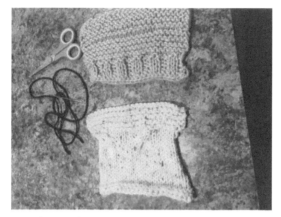

2. Cut a piece of the yarn that matches the color of both pieces and is about twice as long as the pieces (as you can see in the picture below, I chose a different color only to make it easier to follow)

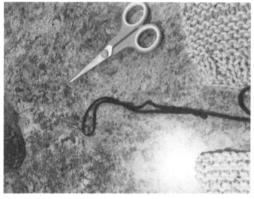

3. Thread the piece through the eye of the knitting needle
4. Place safety pins along the edge to keep the pieces aligned (I didn't use them on these short pieces)

5. With a tail on the yarn go down through the edge of piece A and up into the edge of piece B

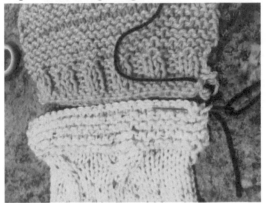

6. Staying along the border that you are trying to match up, pick up a couple of stitches on piece B

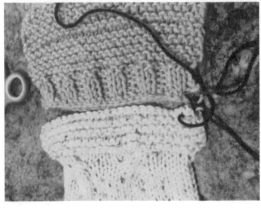

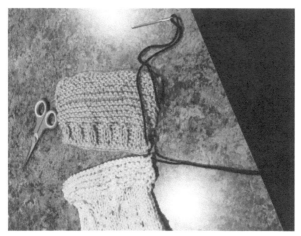

7. Coming back to piece A, starting at the insert mark, pick up a couple of stitches along the border on piece A. They should be about even now.

8. Going back to piece B where the last set of picked up stitches ended, pick up a couple of stitches along the border. Repeat

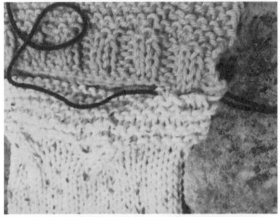

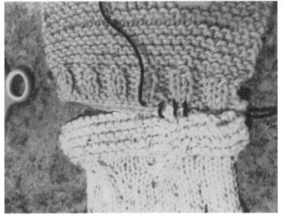

9. Staying along the border on piece A, go to about where the first set of stitches ended and pick up a couple of pieces along the border

10. Continue to repeat 8 and 9 and remove the safety pins as you get to them

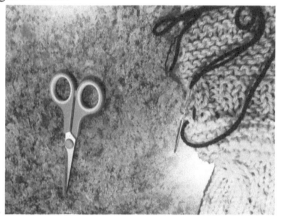

11. Continue until you get the end and pull both ends until its snug. (I flipped it to show what the inside will look like)

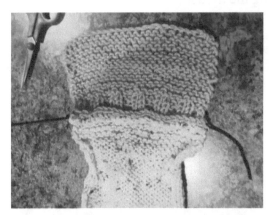

12. When l you get to the end, knot off both ends

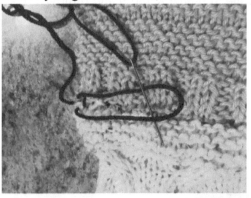

13. Weave the ends in

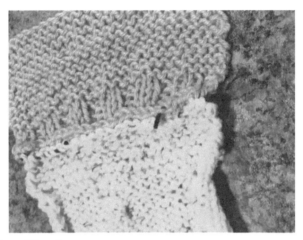

14. Cut off ends

As you can see below, the black string should not show on the outside.

35. ADD ANOTHER COLOR YARN UNNOTICEABLY

In striped patterns, it can be a little tricky. The biggest part is to make sure that you are doing the right stitch on the right side. If you have it correct, what looks like a dotted line will be on the side not seen (wrong side) and the solid line will be on the correct side. If you are not sure, do a few stitches and look at both sides. If it is a blanket or anything else that is seen on both sides, there isn't a way to avoid the dotted line from showing, and in that case, I would suggest that you just stay consistent.

1. At the begging of the right (front) side is where you will want to add the new color. Go into the first stitch the same as you have been doing

2. Pull out about 5-6 inches of the new color and bend it in half making a loop

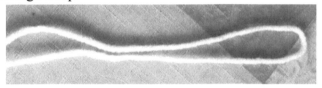

3. Go into the left needle for the necessary stitch just like normal (left knit, right purl)

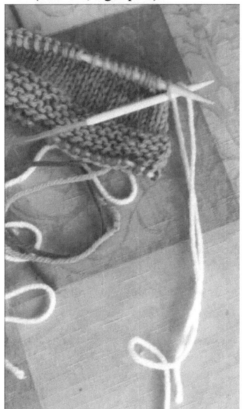

4. When through the stitch wrap the loop around the needle and finish the stitch sliding it off

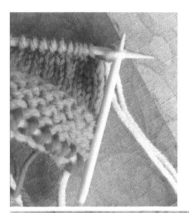

Do the rest of the stitches like normal stitches, go in, yarn over, slide it off

5. Repeat to the end
6. The end of the loop in step 2, is to be knotted and weaved

Back

Front

If this is a scarf, socks, hat, or anything else that doesn't have a large number of stitches and you are planning to do continuous striping, do not detach either yarn. When you finish a stripe, pick up the alternate color, do the stripe, pick up the other color, do the stripe, etc. Yes in the end you will have strings along the edges, but if it has a border that can hide it or they can be cut and weaved in later.

36. ALL STITCHES ON HOLDER

If there are stitches on a stitch holder or a string of yarn, it is done a little differently. If both the front and back neck stitches are on stitch holders or yarn it is a simple process to complete the neck. Starting at one of the shoulders put the end of a need in the stitch. Slowly slide the needle into each stitch that is on the holder or yarn. Once all the stitches are on the needle, remove the stitch holder or cut the yarn and pull it out. You may want to put a marker there if there is a pattern or difference in how the front and back are done.

Some stitch holders will make you take them off of it as you go and I would suggest that you put them onto a double-pointed needle because stitch holder usually makes you remove the stitches from the wrong end first and you will have to slide the stitches to the correct end to proceed. If you are using a cable needle, you can do the same now with the other stitch holder to remove the stitches. Again you may want to put another maker and follow the pattern around the collar and bind off. If you are using long double pointed needles for the neck, you can do the front of the neck in the pattern then the back of the neck, and then sew them together.

37. SOME STITCHES ON A HOLDER, SOME NEED PICK UP

Some patterns will have you do a quantity of stitches and then place them on a stitch holder and finish the row. When you switch the needles in the hands you will have a small number of stitches to work with. This is a shoulder. The pattern will tell you how many rows to do and then bind off. It will then tell you to take a certain number of stitches from the stitch holder or yarn. Again, this is where using the yarn holder is easier because you can cut the yarn at that end, then slip off the quantity needed for the other shoulder and put in another knot for the remaining stitches. If it's on the stitch holder, I would figure out what the neck quantity is and slide that quantity of stitches from one stitch holder to another and put the remaining on the knitting needle s to do the rest of the shoulder pattern.

When you get to the point of doing the neck from this part you will need to do it differently. The pattern should tell you where to start, if it doesn't I would suggest the front left shoulder. Now count to get a rough idea of how many stitches are available and how many the pattern says you need to pick up. Once you know how many for the left and right side, look at the front and back necks to see if you divide that quantity evenly or if there are more needed to be picked up for the backside or the front side. Now that you know about how many you will need to pick up on all four locations, starting at the left should do the pick-up stitches as you did in section 34. Once you get that quantity, knit or purl the stitches from the holder. Again, it is easier to knit them from the yarn and then cut the yarn and pull it out, than to knit them from the stitch holder. Once all of them from the holder is on your needles, do the pick-ups on the other shoulder. If using a cable needle, do the pick up on the necessary back right shoulder, knit the stitches from the holder, and pick up the last stitches. Place a marker and finish the pattern, bind off, and knot and weave in ends. If using straight needles once you get all the second set picked up in the front, do the pattern and bind of, and knot and weave in ends. Then do the same for the back.

38. HOW TO ADD BUTTONHOLES

Buttonholes are pretty simple to add. If it is in the pattern, do knit or purl the requested number of stitches. If it is one of your own, put two safety pins in the area that you would like the hole to be on the next row. Count how many stitches are between the safety pins. When you do the next row and get to the first safety pin do the knit or purl of that one and the next one and then bind the first one-off by the second. If there is more than one, say four stitches between the safety pins, do the next three knit or purl stitches, and bind off again. Continue this until you have reached the last safety pin and then finish the row. Do the next row like a normal row until you get to the first bound off stitch. When you get there do one cast-on stitch if there was only one bind off and you are set. If there were four bind-off stitches, then do four cast-on stitches. Then do the next normal stitch and finish the row. You are all set with a buttonhole.

39. HOW TO ADJUST A SIZE

You may find a pattern that you like, but that it doesn't size appropriate. There are a couple of ways to make adjustments to patterns, some I suggest more than others. You can adjust the needles, the yarn, and the numbers. I put them in the order of suggestion. For example, if you need to make it smaller than the pattern states and the pattern says that you use a size 8 needle, you can adjust that to a size 4 and it will be a lot smaller. If that is still not enough, adjust the weight of the yarn. Change the yarn from the weight from 4 to 2 or add another skein of yarn so there are two skeins at once (see section 45). Hopefully, between these three adjustments, you can get the correct gauge. The only other one is to mathematically recalculate. If it is a pattern that doesn't have special stitches or styles within adjustments are easier, but still, have to be removed or added from the correct locations and ALL locations. If there is a design in the pattern, it is the most difficult and I still have difficulties calculating them correctly every time.

For any of these adjustments, I would suggest that you do gauges. So if it says size 8 and you use the 4, do a gauge with the same amount of stitches and measure to see how much of a difference there is. Then if you need more you can do another gauge with a smaller needle or a smaller weight yarn and hopefully, you won't need to calculate.

40. CHARTS AVAILABLE

There are charts available in books and on the internet that can assist you in deciding the supplies that you will need when working without a pattern. These charts will give you what and how to measure, how much yarn you will need to purchase based measurements and on the size and the weight of the yarn, and what size needles are recommended. Also, keep in mind that in some countries sizes run smaller, so try to find charts that are in the measurements that you know and understand. Again, even going based on the suggestions; I would still do a gauge.

41. DROPPING ROWS AND PICKING UP

There will come times when you will need to drop some completed rows. This could be because you find that you missed a section of the pattern, don't like the way it is turning out, or any other reason that would make you go back an entire row or more.

Before:

1. Slide-out the needle that is holding the stitches

2. Pull out the necessary rows to get to the last correct row

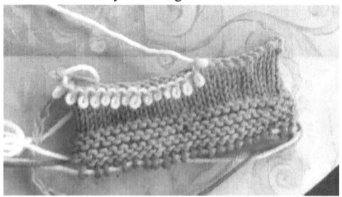

3. Slide the needle back into the project. If you know how many stitches you should have, count them to see that you pick them all up. If you miss some proceed with 4 but see section 41.

4. Go ahead and follow your pattern, however, watch for twisted stitches. You will notice them. They just don't look and feel right when you go to do the stitch. If you notice it, turn the stitch around on the right needle and proceed.

42. HOW TO FIX A DROPPED STITCH

A dropped stitch is one that you might notice right off the bat and one that you may not notice until many rows later. One of the great things about knitting is that if you find that you dropped a stitch or did an incorrect stitch (ex. did a purl, should have been a knit), you can fix it and not have to pull any stitches out. If you are on a pattern that is stockinette stitch flat (knit side) or all puffy (purl side) then this is very simple. However, if it is just continuous knit or continuous purl on both sides or patterns within, it gets tricky.

When working on the knit (flat) side of a stockinette stitch part of a project it can be very simple to fix a stitch if you know how to crochet. In crocheting, you do the chain to start s project and on the knit side of a fix, you use the chain stitch to fix.

1. Knit over to the column where the mistake or the dropped stitch is located

2. Slide that stitch off the needle

3. Slowly separate the rows until you get to the error and make sure to have it pulled out too

4. Take your crochet hook and put in through the stitch below it

5. Now do a crochet-like chain stitch to the string across for the above row, put the string under the head of the crochet hook and pull it through

6. Go to the row above and repeat until you get to the top and last row

7. Then put it back on the knitting needle, check to see that it is put on in the right direction (it looks like the others) you may need to turn it around.

When working on a purl (puffy) section of a stockinette stitch, it can be a little more tricky, but still fairly simple.

1. Purl over to the column where the mistake or the dropped stitch is located

2. Slide that stitch off the needle

3. Slowly separate the rows until you get to the error and make sure to have it pulled out too

4. Take your crochet hook and put in through the stitch below it, but instead of from the bottom, through the top under the row above.

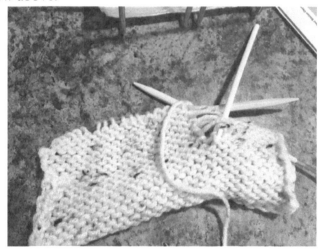

5. Now do a crochet chain stitch to the string across for the above row, put the string under the head of the crochet hook and pull it through

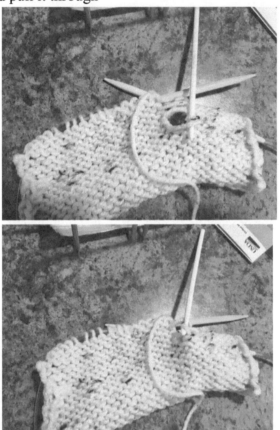

6. Go to the row above and repeat until you get to the top and last row

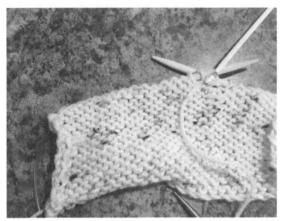

7. Then put it back on the knitting needle, check to see that it is put on in the right direction (it looks like the others) you may need to turn it around.

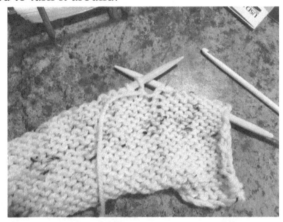

You can flip the project upside down, to make it easier to see what you are doing if the project is a size that allows easy movement. Another simpler note is that if you flip the project over, you can just do the knit fix, which I find much simpler.

Now if you are working with a project that has just knit or just purl, so that it all looks the same on either side, a fix is most tricky. You will have to do both of what is above on the correct row and keep alternating for the rows. If you spread out these rows on either side you will see that even though you are continuously doing the same stitch on the pattern because you are flipping it over, it alternates. Think of it how when you stand face to face with someone and you both lift your right-hand, it's the opposite of yours. If you want it the same on the other side you have to do the opposite. It's the same here.

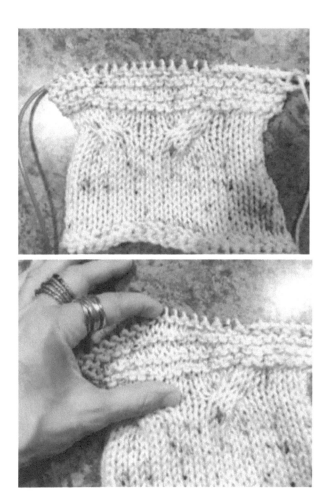

1. Knit or purl over to the column where the mistake or the dropped stitch is located
2. Slide that stitch off the needle
3. Slowly separate the rows until you get to the error and make sure to have it pulled out too

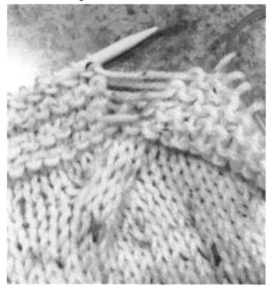

4. Spread the rows out so you can see clearly if that is a knit or purl stitch

   If it is a knit stitch, do a chain stitch to the string across for the above row, put the string under the head of the crochet hook and pull it through

5. Pull the crochet hook out
6. Do a purl fix, put your crochet hook through the stitch below it, from the top and under the row above, do a crochet chain, pulling the through

7. Pull the crochet hook out
8. Do a knit stitch fix

9. Pull the crochet hook out
10. Do a purl stitch fix

11. Continue to until you get to the top and last row

12. Then put it back on the knitting needle, check to see that it is put on in the right direction (it looks like the others) you may need to turn it around

43. KNITTING VS CROCHETING

I have mentioned crocheting a lot. So at this point, I would like to do some comparisons for you that I think would be helpful or informational. To know basic crocheting, the chain is very helpful in knitting. However, if you know how to do a single crochet stitch or more, you can use it for decorations on projects, putting pieces together, or combine crochet and knitting in projects. I find that crochet projects tend to be thicker even if with the same size needles and yarn. However, one of the biggest differences I have noticed and what has made it the difference for me is if there is an error. I have just shown you how simple a fix can be on an error or dropped stitch in knitting, even if it was 50 rows ago. However, through my years of yarn working, I have not found a way in crochet to fix that same error 50 rows ago, without pulling out all 50 rows. I'm human and know I get distracted, misread a pattern, and still to this day

129

have to fix mistakes from missing or dropping a stitch. I much rather fix it by the column than pull all those hours out. Therefore, if I am going to make a blanket and decide to crochet, I do blocks and put them aside and sew them together.

44. HOW TO ADJUST PATTERN DIRECTIONS FOR NEEDLE PREFERENCES

You may find that you like to work with some yarns and some equipment more than others. Like I have said before, I prefer the cable needles. Yes, one reason is that it allows me to work in smaller spaces, but allows me to adjust the way I do patterns too. For example, a sweater is one that I adjust and do the biggest parts differently by using a cable needle. Most sweater patterns will give you the directions for the front of the sweater, the back of the sweater, each arm (same), neck, and sew it together. I do as little sewing as possible. I just think my work looks better and I can try it on as I proceed to see if it is the lengths I want. So here is what I change.

1. Calculate the number of stitches necessary for both the front and the back of the sweater
2. Cast-on the quantity of the front
3. Put a marker
4. Cast-on the quantity for the back
5. Put a marker
6. Follow the pattern for the front to a marker, then follow the pattern for the back to the other marker *** (see below)
7. Follow the pattern until it gets to the point where there is a difference in what is done on the front and what is done on the back. This is usually at the armpit or maybe a pattern

8. Slide the stitches for the back onto a string of yarn and knot it
9. Follow the pattern for the front until complete, leaving the neck stitches on a yarn holder instead of binding off
10. Slide the stitches from the string of yarn back to the needles and follow the pattern for the back until complete, leaving the neck stitches on a yarn holder instead of binding off
11. Sew the shoulders together
12. Pick up the stitches for a sleeve, starting at the bottom of the armpit and go up and around on either side
13. Reverse the directions of how many stitches I should have and slowly decrease to the wrist instead of increase to the shoulder following the pattern. Where it says to increase, I decrease and try it on as I go to make the sleeve the length I want
14. The sewing of the sleeve will be the same except you will not have to connect it at the top too, just sewing the sides together right down to the split. It's the underside of the sleeve
15. Repeat for the other sleeve
16. See how many stitches are necessary for the neck and if necessary add more follow the directions from section 36 if you need more than what is on the strings of yarn. Otherwise, follow the pattern.

***Keep in mind that if you are doing say a sweater and you do continuous knitting or purling on cable needles (not turning around, just going in a big circle) that if the pattern says to knit a row, then turn and purl a row, just keep knitting. If purl a row and then, then knit a row on a circular need keep doing the purl. It wants a stockinette stitch (St st) pattern, all smooth or all bumpy.

You should be all set.

If you like the multiple needles, you can do the same as above, but with multiple double-pointed needles. You will do the same for the most part, but you will have to be more careful about keeping your quantity of stitches evenly divided among the needles. I would also suggest keeping caps on all of the needles, not in use, and keep the cap on the base end of the need in use. Another note is that keeping the markers may be more difficult on the double-pointed needles and until you get a lot of practice, knowing where to start when you pick them back up can be tricky. However, for these needles, the neck will be easier to add any additional stitches if necessary, but try to add them equally among the needles.

45. YARN WEIGHT DIFFERENCE IMPACTS

The weight in yarn can range drastically. The weight 0, zero, is a Lace yarn as mentioned about and I did go up to a size 7, which is a Jumbo weight yarn. I don't want to give the impression that these are the only weights available. These weights can be viewed as how big around the yarn is in strand thickness. There are yarns available that are 8.5 are larger. These yarns are more for arm knitting. If you've made it this far, you can arm knit too. It can be done as using your arms as the knitting needles or flat out on a table knitting. I have placed some links at the end for you to see for how to knit with this type of yarn. I liked the outcome from the table knitting, but I have very muscular arms so that made a difference in the size of the stitches. I also think it would depend on what you are trying to make. If making a blanket with that thick of yarn and you do it on your arms, you will have to do strips and sew them together, however, if you do it on a table you can make it as wide as you want at the start and not have to sew them together. If you do need to sew this yarn together, stitches will be the same, but with your hands and fingers weaving the yarn in, not a needle. See the links at the end for videos and pictures of how to knit with this yarn. I have done it and enjoyed it and the ending results.

46. TWO SKEINS ONCE

Although when looking at a beautiful finished project of multiple colors may seem like more work, it isn't. The work and the patterns are all done the same. The difference is that you will do everything the same, but with the two skeins of yarn simultaneously. When you make your loops to start, make one with each skein of yarn, and put the needle through both. It won't matter which one you go through first unless the pattern tells you otherwise. You will do all the stitches the same. You will go through both cast-on stitches at the same time, yarn over with both yarns, come back through both cast-on stitches, and slide both on the needle. It will now look like you have four stitches on the needle, but actually, you only have two with each color, so two sets. Repeat. It will be the same when you do stitches, but you will pick up two from the left needle, yarn over with both yarns, and slide off two onto the right needle. In the end, these projects tend to be thicker. So if you have a pattern that you are thinking about using two scans of yarn simultaneously, again do gauge. It may not be exactly half as many stitches needed and the gauge will help you figure that out.

Here are some pictures to show you that it is all done the same. When you get to the second row, make sure to pick up both stitches of yarn or in my case, both colors.

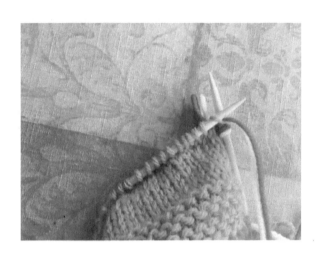

47. HOW AND WHERE TO FIND PATTERNS

In today's world, it is very easy to be overwhelmed with where and how to find the pattern that you are looking for. Therefore, I am going to give you some suggestions for different places to look at and the good points and bad points of each. There or more options available than I will cover, but this will give you a start. Some of the most common are at stores like Michael's, Joanne Fabrics, Walmart, etc., but there is also, Pinterest, Amazon/eBay, and yarn or pattern websites, and of course, you can find some on YouTube.

Let's start with well-known stores such as Michael's, Joanne Fabrics, Walmart, and other stores that have arts and crafts materials. The good points about these stores are that you could start from having absolutely nothing and walk out with everything you need for your project. The first thing to do is pick the pattern, find the supplies that it says you need, get the correct weight, and quantity of yarn with the same dye lot numbers, and you are all set.

The bad point is that sometimes these stores may not have enough of the skeins of yarn that you need and another one is that they do tend to be more expensive.

Pinterest.com is great to help you find the pattern that you are looking for. They have such a vast array of different styles of the same projects, it is hard to pick only one. The patterns can be broke down in groups of beginner to expert levels for searches, they can be sorted by colors, styles, etc. and most of the patterns are free. You can find what you want and if you find more than one, you can start an account and save them for future projects. There are no fees or obligations to the account and you can end it any time. There is a vast array to choose from pocketbooks, slippers, baskets, knitting socks, supply bags, dog sweaters, etc. I found many patterns instigated my imagination to create my own and I found that Pinterest has other areas that are of interest to me such as cooking that I can save on another "Pin".

However, there are bad points to Pinterest when looking for a project. Sometimes the finished product you want to make is displayed under patterns, but it is already made and for sale by a vendor. Sometimes the patterns are in a different language, and sometimes they are not complete directions and occasionally, lead you to sites that are not free. You also will have to go to another website to purchase the supplies.

Amazon.com and *eBay.com* are the same, but different and if you have used them both frequently, you know why I say that. Either site gives you the option of being more like in a store like mentioned above. You can go on from having absolutely nothing and check out with everything you need for your project. It would be just like walking into a store and picking the pattern, finding the supplies, getting the yarn, and checking out at the register. Here you will know if they have all of the quantities of the supplies that you will need at that time of purchase and can get it sorted to only show you the ones that have sufficient quantities and they do tend to less expensive.

The bad point is that the colors may appear differently on the screen compared to when received and that can be because of the resolutions on your computer or the pictures posted on the website. Another bad point is waiting for the supplies. They may all come together, but some may take longer and be on backorder.

Yarn and pattern websites both have good points and bad points. Some Yarn sites give you unbeatable deals on yarn. It can be specials to promote, sales on new, and, of course, sales on the discontinued or remaining balance. Some yarns will also have free patterns available on the backside of the label and you will know how much is available. Pattern websites tend to be the same. They may have patterns that are at a cost, some that are on sale, and some that are discontinued and free. Some pattern sites have contracts with yarn manufactures to give you links to them or they have yarn of their own. There is usually customer service available for questions at either of these types of sites and some of the sites also have package deals for other supplies and suppliers.

The bad sides are the same as the others, the colors may appear differently on the screen compared to when received and that can be because of the resolutions on your computer or the pictures posted on the website. Supplies may all come together, but some may take longer and be on backorder.

YouTube.com is going to be mentioned here for patterns. I say this because you can find a pattern for free on YouTube that has a video to watch throughout the entire project. If you live on a cell phone, these patterns will work fine for you to save and return to the spot you stopped at as long as you are a member of YouTube. They have videos that are usually very well explained and demonstrated.

However, they do not tend to supply you with access to the find the supplies that you need, and it may not tell you the correct weight and quantity of yarn with the same dye lot numbers to get, and how to adjust pattern sizes.

48. WHAT TO DO WITH SCRAP YARN

I mentioned when we were looking at the supplies pack that if you have a small ball of yarn leftover, put it in your supplies bag for markers, stitch holders, etc. However, if the amount on the skein is too much for that, there are other options. There are patterns available to use up yarn on Pinterest and Youtube. You can also use it for borders on projects. Maybe make blocks and save them for one big blanket. How about making something for a baby, a small dog, a hat, or use it for striping! There are so many options I just want you to be aware that unless it is an untouched skein of yarn leftover from a finished project that you can return, keep it. The options available are unlimited.

49. DIFFERENT STITCH PATTERNS

There are all different kinds of patterns that you can do now that you know how to knit and purl. Some of them can be simple single and double ribbed like the wrist, others will look like suspended dots. However, some patterns use these stitches to make designs. Some of these that I have seen over the years is the Lattice, Daisy Flower, St. John's Wort, and Scroll Lace. There are links at the end to show you what these different stitches look like, but there are many more.

50. HELPFUL HINTS

Over the years I have learned a few things or created a few helpful hints of my own. I have mentioned some of these helpful hints along the way. Here I am going to add some and mention or restate some from above. I wish I knew some of these when I started, it would have saved me a lot of wasted work and tear outs.

- Always do a gauge if you are following a pattern or have a specific measurement that you want in the ending result. This gauge will give you the measurements with the supplies you are working with and let you know if they need adjustments. These adjustments can include the size of the yarn, the weight of the yarn, and the quantity of stitches.
- Read entire directions before deciding to do a project. Some projects start easy and get more complicated. They are often labeled by difficulty ratings. Some patterns have areas that you may have to look up the terms. If the pattern is from another country the verbiage may be different, but mean the same as what you know.
- When you have completed a row and switch the hands the needles are in and do the first couple stitches, make sure to pull the yarn tight and keep it taut. Once you do about four stitches it doesn't matter, but if you don't the first stitch you do will hang loosely and it will make it more difficult to sew it together nice and neat.
- Once you get the swing of knitting, don't bind off stitches that will need to be created again such as in the neck of a sweater. Why bind off stitches only to cast them back on later. Put them on extra yarn or a stitch holder.
- Put markers in between patterns. When there is a pattern being used and you have to change what pattern you are doing, put in a marker. So if you are K2, P2, K2, P2,

KKKKK, then P3, K3, P3, K3, PPPPP, repeat; put a marker after the last P in PPPPP. This way you will know to change when you come across it again on the next row.

- Use sticky notes to keep track of where you are on the patterns, tally marks for counts, notes to yourself, etc.
- You can create your ways to do things like I've done and mentioned or ones that you create that work. Whatever makes knitting more fun for you, do it.

51. GOOD FOR MEDITATION

I have been knitting for about 20 years now. For me it is relaxing. I sometimes use it as a form of meditation, but I can enjoy doing a knitting project while I am doing numerous other things. I can watch a movie while I knit, take it to one of the kids' ball games, or even work on it in the passenger seat on a trip across the country. You name it, I have probably done it. I find it to be relaxing when I am under stress or just the perfect timer when I'm baking. I do it more in the wintertime when there are limited entertainment options to do inside and still feel the successful accomplishments.

52. GROUP PROJECTS OR TIME

Some projects can be done in groups or you can create group time for a project. When I instruct knitting, I reserve a location and each person does their first project. We work on each section individually at the same time. For example, when my classes start, I teach everyone in the class how to cast-on and how to do the knit stitch. They work on that for the first week and then in the second week I teach them how to do the purl stitch. They work on that for the second week and in the third week, I show them how to do the dropped stitch fix and the bind off. They can then decide if they would like to start the scarf over, find another project to have me help them with pattern reading, or continue. Some of the students will do the bind off.

There are group projects around that they can donate their practice work to and depending on the size. Some public places collect them and knit them together to make blankets. They can be used to make coasters, parts of hats, and even baby slippers if they are folded and sewn together correctly. Some of the small skeins of yarn are used in group projects just to make decorations like flowers or eyes for knitted stuffed animals.

53. OR WHOM TO KNIT

If you are like me, you do not have little kids or grandchildren to knit for, so who do I make that cute baby sweater and hat for? Hospitals have stores and babies. I make cute outfits, lap blankets, hats, coasters, etc. and donate them to the hospital stores. Maybe that family member that came from out of state to see someone needs a quick gift. Don't forget the cancer centers are always looking for hats and blankets. There are also churches, homeless shelters, foster care, abuse shelters, schools, animal shelters, nursing homes, etc. the list just goes on for places to share your artwork.

If you have made it this far…. I have to thank you! It has been a joy to share one of my favorite hobbies. If you have questions, I do have a Facebook Author Page and an Amazon Author Page with my current publications and more to come!

Next, you will see some of my completed projects that I have created for myself or donated to give you some ideas of what YOU can now do!

REFERENCES:

5 Steps to Switch to Double Pointed Knitting Needles. By Kristen McDonnell. Retrieved on July 22, 2020 from: https://www.studioknitsf.com/how-to-knit-on-dpns-switch-to-double-pointed-knitting-needles/?utm_medium=social&utm_source=pinterest&utm_campaign=tailwind_smartloop&utm_content=smartloop&utm_term=35878034

BLANKETS – BLOCKS, STRIPS, CABLE NEEDLES, ETC. BORDER STYLE AND NEEDLE SIZE

Coloured Baby Cot Blanket Knit in Strips Aran/ DK Knitting Pattern. Retrieved on July 22, 2020 from: https://www.ebay.com/itm/Coloured-Baby-Cot-Blanket-Knit-in-Strips-Aran-DK-Knitting-Pattern-/372246608234

Connect super chunky chenille yarn. BeCozi. Retrieved on July 17, 2020 from: https://www.youtube.com/watch?v=-813pscMb18

Continental Knitting:

Diamond Lattice Knitting Stitch, from Knitting Kingdom, Retrieved on July, 20, 2020 from: https://www.knittingkingdom.com/diamond-lattice-knitting-stitch/

Different stitch patterns (Lattice, Daisy Flower, St. John's Wort, Scroll Lace)

DOUBLE POINTED NEEDLES HAT

Easy Daisy Knit Flower Pattern, from All Free Knitting, Retrieved on July, 20, 2020 from: https://www.allfreeknitting.com/Knit-Accessories/Easy-Daisy-Knit-Flower-Pattern

Google Crochet Borders. Retrieved on July 22, 2020 from: https://www.google.com/search?q=crochet+borders&tbm=isch&

ved=2ahUKEwjE1sLd0ePqAhVGON8KHYm-CV8Q2-
cCegQIABAA&oq=croc+borders&gs_lcp=CgNpbWcQARgAM
gYIABAHEB4yBggAEAcQHjIGCAAQBxAeMgYIABAHEB4
yBggAEAcQHjIGCAAQBxAeMgYIABAHEB4yBggAEAcQHj
IGCAAQBxAeMgYIABAHEB5QxeIFWKfpBWD79gVoAHA
AeACAAVWIAZcCkgEBNJgBAKABAaoBC2d3cy13aXotaW1
nwAEB&sclient=img&ei=5qUZX8TLH8bw_AaJ_ab4BQ&bih=
999&biw=1189

Google Knitted Borders. Retrieved on July 22, 2020 from:
https://www.google.com/search?source=univ&tbm=isch&q=knit
ted+borders&sa=X&ved=2ahUKEwiL4Iix0ePqAhW_lHIEHWF
oCWMQsAR6BAgFEAE&biw=1189&bih=999

How to Knit if You're Left-handed, by Sara E. White, June 17,
2019. Retrieved on June 27, 2020 from
https://www.thesprucecrafts.com/im-left-handed-how-do-i-knit-
2116243

How to Purl Left-handed (Copyright 1997-2020), Retrieved on June
27, 2020 from: https://cyberseams.com/knitting-left-
handed/how-to-purl-left-handed/

How to Purl Left-handed Video. By All Free Knitting. Retrieved on
June 27, 2020 from: https://www.allfreeknitting.com/Knitting-
Tutorials/how-to-purl-left-handed-video

How-to: Arm Knit a Blanket, Yarn Fix-up, Copyright 2015-2020.
Retrieved on July 17 2020, from: http://yarnfix.com/arm-knit-a-
blanket/

In The Loop Knitting, Afghans in Sections Knitting Patterns.
Retrieved on July 22, 2020 from:
https://intheloopknitting.com/afghans-in-sections-knitting-
patterns/

Knit Like Granny, (Copyright 2020), Retrieved on June 25, 2020
from: https://knitlikegranny.com/yarn-types/

Knitting Needle Sizes and Conversion Chart, (Copyright 2020),
Retrieved on June 25, 2020 from
https://sheepandstitch.com/library/knitting-needle-sizes-
conversion-chart/

Learn How to Knit in the Continental Style, The Spruce Crafts.
Retrieved on July 20, 2020 from:
https://www.thesprucecrafts.com/continental-knit-stitch-2116508

Left-hand Knitting Tutorial for Beginners, Retrieved on June 27,
2020 from: https://www.youtube.com/watch?v=OhiKp9Y7cgM

Mama In a Stitch, Easy Native Stripes Knit Blanket/Throw.
Retrieved on July 22, 2020, from:
https://www.mamainastitch.com/easy-native-stripes-knit-
blanket-throw/

Scroll Lace, Knitting Stitch Patterns.com. Retrieved on July, 20,
2020 from:
https://www.knittingstitchpatterns.com/2015/11/scroll-lace-
stitch.html

South Paw Recommendations:

St. John's Wort Knitting Stitch Pattern, by Knitting Bee (Copyright
June 17, 2013). Retrieved on July 20, 2020, from:
https://www.knitting-bee.com/knitting-stitch-library/lace-
stitches/st-johns-wort-knitting-stitch-pattern

Yarn Weight Difference Impacts for arm knitting:

READ OTHER

50 THINGS TO KNOW

BOOKS

50 Things to Know

Stay up to date with new releases on Amazon:
  https://amzn.to/2VPNGr7

Mailing List: Join the 50 Things to Know
  Mailing List to Learn About New Releases

50 Things to Know

Please leave your honest review of this book on Amazon and Goodreads. We appreciate your positive and constructive feedback. Thank you.

Made in United States
Troutdale, OR
09/22/2024